Madam and Nun and 1001

What Is a Palindrome?

To my niece, Hannah
—B.P.C.

Palindrome:
A word, phrase, sentence, or number that is the same when read forward or backward

Madam and Nun and 1001

What Is a Palindrome?

by Brian P. Cleary

illustrations by Brian Gable

M MILLBROOK PRESS / MINNEAPOLIS

A palindrome's
a word or number,
sentence, phrase, or name

that—when it's read backward—
is spelled and said the same.

HANNAH is a palindrome, like MOM and DAD and SIS,

BIB

and NOON

and SOLOS.

Are you catching on to this?

WOW! There's MADAM, GAG, and BOB, REFER, and many more words.

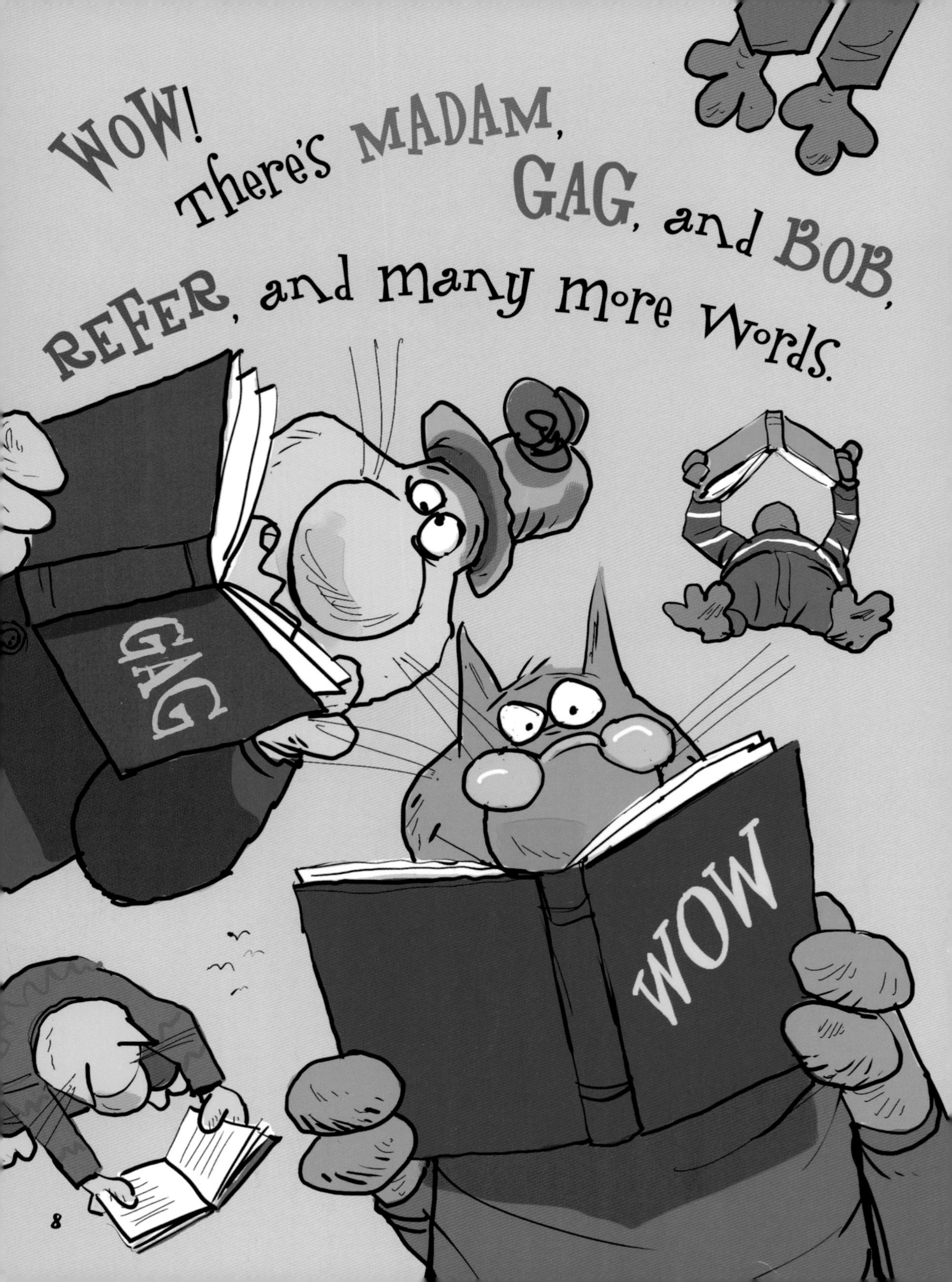

All are spelled the same if they're read backwards or read forwards!

other palindromes are RADAR,

CIVIC,

RACE CAR,

NUN,

PULL-UP,

LEVEL,

EYE,

and DEED,

and 1991.

Some are long like ROTAVATOR,

KAYAK, also REDDER.

This kind gets more challenging with every extra letter.

TEST SET is a palindrome,

like EWE

or A TOYOTA,

and soft drinks
some will say are POP
While others call them soda.

TOOT and MUM are palindromes, like TENET and AHA,

as well as this whole question here:
"WAS IT A CAT I SAW?"

17

WAS IT A

See how, with that question, you can read it left to right?

CAT I SAW?

But if you read it backward,
it's the same words you'd recite!

You might see them at the store or even in graffiti

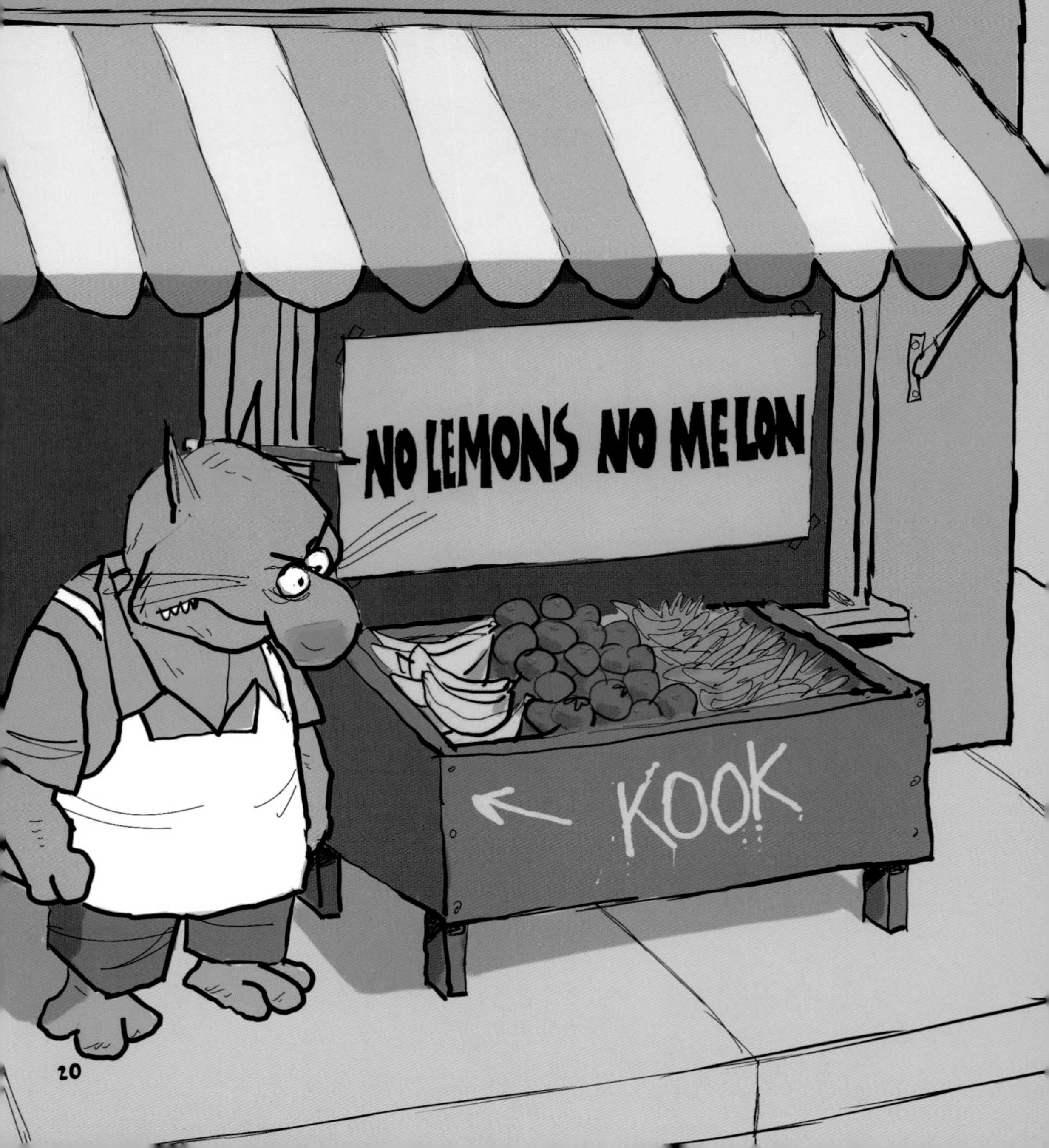

or on a sign that cautions grown-ups not to be too speedy.

Palindromes can be commands

or ask a simple question.

They could show up in proper nouns or even a suggestion.

Some are ancient, etched in stone, and others soon could vanish.

Some are Portuguese or Greek or Finnish, French, or Spanish.

Does it take work to think of them?
Why, sure, but **NOT A TON.**

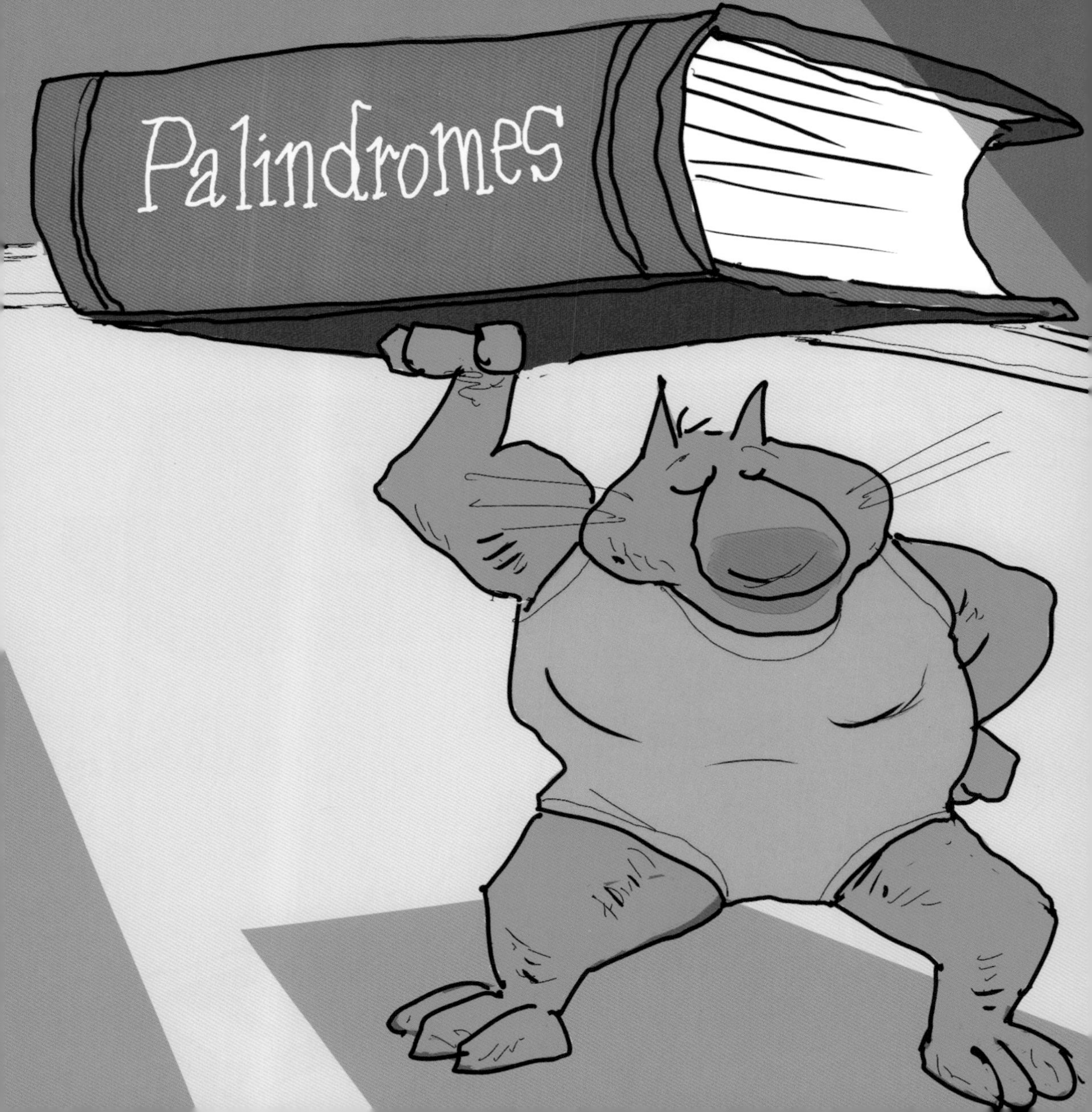

So, whether you're a TOT or teacher,
find a friend and play,

and put the "pal" in palindrome.
You've made one? Holler, "YAY!"

So, what is a palindrome?
Do you know?

Find activities, games, and more at
www.brianpcleary.com

ABOUT THE AUTHOR & ILLUSTRATOR

BRIAN P. CLEARY is the author of the best-selling Words Are CATegorical® series as well as the Math Is CATegorical®, Food Is CATegorical™, Animal Groups Are CATegorical™, Adventures in Memory™, and Sounds Like Reading® series. He has also written Do You Know Dewey? Exploring the Dewey Decimal System, Six Sheep Sip Thick Shakes: And Other Tricky Tongue Twisters, and several other books. Mr. Cleary lives in Cleveland, Ohio.

BRIAN GABLE is the illustrator of many Words Are CATegorical® books and the Math Is CATegorical® series. Mr. Gable also works as a political cartoonist for the Globe and Mail newspaper in Toronto, Canada.

Millbrook Press
A division of Lerner Publishing Group, Inc.
241 First Avenue North
Minneapolis, MN 55401 U.S.A.

Website address: www.lernerbooks.com

Main body text set in RandumTEMP 35/48.
Typeface provided by House Industries.

Library of Congress Cataloging-in-Publication Data

Cleary, Brian P., 1959–
    Madam and nun and 1001 : what is a palindrome? / by Brian P. Cleary ; illustrations by Brian Gable.
      p.   cm. — (Words are CATegorical)
    ISBN 978–0–7613–4919–8 (lib. bdg. : alk. paper)
    1. Palindromes—Juvenile literature. I. Gable, Brian, 1949—, ill. II. Title. III. Title: Madam and nun and one thousand and one.
    PN6371.5.C53 2012
    793.734—dc23   2011044856

Manufactured in the United States of America
1 — DP — 7/15/12